BRIEFINGS

£2·99

The Silk Road

Church and mission in Turkey,
Iran and Central Asia

OM
publishing

Copyright © 2001 Glenn Myers

OM Publishing is an imprint of Paternoster Publishing,
P.O. Box 300, Carlisle, Cumbria, CA3 0QS, U.K.

03 02 01 00 99 98   7 6 5 4 3 2 1

The right of Glenn Myers to be identified as the Author of this Work has been
asserted by him in accordance with Copyright, Designs and Patents Act 1988.

*All rights reserved. No part of this publication may be reproduced, stored in
a retrieval system, or transmitted in any form or by any means, electric,
mechanical, photocopying, recording or otherwise, without the prior
permission of the publisher or a license permitting restricted copying.
In the U.K. such licenses are issued by the Copyright Licensing Agency,
90, Tottenham Court Road, London W1P 9HE.*

British Library Cataloguing in Publication Data
A catalogue record for this book is available from the British Library

ISBN 1-85078-376-4

Designed by Christopher Lawther, Teamwork, Lancing, West Sussex.
Typeset by WestKey Ltd, Falmouth, Cornwall.
Produced by Jeremy Mudditt Publishing Services, Carlisle,
and printed and bound in Great Britain by
Tyndale Press, Lowestoft, Suffolk.

CONTENTS

This book was produced from the International Research and UK Publications departments of WEC International.

WEC International is an interdenominational missions agency aiming to bring the Christian gospel to the remaining unevangelised peoples of the world. WEC is made up of over 1900 workers from 43 nations serving Christ together in over 60 countries.

Start here

This booklet tells the remarkable story of the Church in the Turkic and Persian worlds, especially over the last two decades. It is no more than a sketch. We consider the three main areas in turn: the former Soviet Central Asian states; Turkey; and Iran. We also discuss briefly Turkic and Persian peoples elsewhere.

My thanks to the many people who gave interviews or provided source material or criticism. Some people are mentioned in the endnotes; most preferred their names to be left out. I'm also very grateful to the team that has helped produce these books over the years: my colleagues in WEC International, especially the International Research Office staff; Jeremy Mudditt; and Daphne Spraggett who has skewered many an inelegant sentence with her red pen. The picture in the Persian World chapter is courtesy of Elam Ministries; the cover picture is courtesy of OM; the rest are from the WEC archives. All are copyright. Special thanks, as ever, to Cordelia and our children.

A WORD ON WORDS

Our cultural need for neat categories serves us poorly when we consider the diverse and intermingled peoples discussed in this book. Every category we use (Turkic, Persian, folk Muslim, Sufi, Sunni, Russified, westernized, even 'Christian') overflows when confronted with the wonderful anarchic diversity of actual human beings. Here, however, are some of the words I've used:

I use 'Central Asia' in this book as shorthand for the former Soviet states of the Caucasus (Armenia, Georgia, Azerbaijan) and of Central Asia (Kazakhstan, Kyrgyzstan, Tajikistan, Turkmenistan, and Uzbekistan), as well as Xinjiang province of China. Xinjiang province is the 'East Turkestan' of old literature. ('West Turkestan' corresponds to the rest of Central Asia, as far as the Caspian Sea.) I have said little directly about what is happening in Xinjiang because of the extreme sensitivity of the region. However, the peoples and trends found in Xinjiang have close parallels with the rest of Central Asia. And despite severe restrictions, the Church is growing.

'Turkish' in this book specifically refers to people from Turkey. 'Turkic' is wider: it refers to Turkic-speaking peoples from whatever country.

The 'Persian world' occupies a wide part of Western Asia (see the affinity groups map at the back). I have tried to discuss some of this world's uniqueness in the chapter on Iran. Turkic and Persian peoples are very different but are also inter-mingled in a complex way in Central Asia, Iran, Turkey and beyond. Cultural ties sometimes provide one set of links, recent history another. Tajikistan (part of the Persian world), for example, is now part of the story of Soviet Central Asia; Azerbaijanis (part of the Turkic world) form a significant minority within Iran and share that country's distinctive recent history; and so on.

I have not discussed Afghanistan. This too has a large Persian element and a smaller Turkic element but may be better considered along with Pakistan, Bangladesh and North India in some (possible) future *Briefing*.

Glenn Myers
Cambridge, December 2000

Central Asia

The desert, steppe and mountain ranges of Central Asia form a space as wide as an ocean, and almost as empty. Central Asia is the size of India, or half as big again as the Mediterranean Sea, but relatively few people live here – only about 65m of them. Some are nomads, guiding flocks and herds between annual feeding grounds; others cluster in the oases or fertile valleys that speckle the lean plains like tiny islands and reefs.

Mostly, though – in what is claimed to be a crowded world – what you find in Central Asia is emptiness. Travelling by train across the Kazakh steppe to China, you can see the same flat view out of the window both before a good night's sleep and afterwards: the train moves, the landscape doesn't.

TOO LARGE TO MANAGE

Clustered around the shoreline of Central Asia are European, Turkish, Arab, Persian, Indian, and Chinese civilisations. Most of these have tried to control Central Asia at one time or another. All have found Central Asia too large and empty to digest. Central Asia is easy to capture, hard to keep.

The events of the early 1990s, when the former Soviet Union lost its Central Asian territories, were just the latest in an unending story of failed attempts at possession: Russia's empire could no more incorporate Central Asia's vastness than could the empires of Alexander the Great or the Mongols.

A TURKIC PEOPLE

Old books refer to Central Asia as 'Turkestan'. What has endured among the peoples of Central Asia through the turbulent centuries is their Turkic-ness. This is a Turkic-ness of horses and cattle; mutton and mare's milk; close-knit families and close-woven carpets; flat bread and open skies; yurts and poetry. The Turkic peoples of Central Asia still speak a swatch of closely related, though distinct, languages. A Turkish native speaker from Ankara, in Turkey, can be understood quite well in Ashgabat, Turkmenistan and may claim to have a good idea of what is going on even in Urumqi in China's northwest.

They're a famous family. Many of the famous peoples of Central Asian history – Huns, Mongols, Tatars – have Turkic roots. Further west, Turks have ruled the Arab world across most of its length and for much of its history. As a result you find large Turkic communities as far west as Bulgaria and Germany, as far south as Iran, as far north as Siberia. They originated near the Altai mountains on the Kazakh/Chinese/Mongolian borders; they have come a long way since.

TODAY

Today is not the finest hour for the Turkic world. Much of it is emerging from Communism's shadow. All of it is struggling with globalisation. From east to west you can see people un- or under-employed, having mostly swapped the skies and flocks for cramped apartments and clapped-out factories. You can find old people from Central Asian families begging on the streets – a scandal in a set of cultures that through the millennia have revered the aged.

Yet at the same time something is happening among them that has not happened for more than a thousand years. Simultaneously across Central Asia, and across the wider Turkic world from Bulgaria to Xinjiang, as sudden as the end of an eclipse, people are finding new life in Christ. Thousands already have. More will.

The story of these peoples' turn to respond to the Lord Jesus is a story mostly of the past twenty years – and indeed mainly of the past ten. But to tell it properly we need to go a long way further back ... to a certain Wudi, 'the Son of Heaven', fabled Emperor of China a hundred years before Christ.

– 1 –
The Silk Road

GLOBAL TRADING AND DESIGNER CLOTHES

In 138 BC Chinese Emperor Han Wudi was having problems with one of China's ancient foes, an invading Turkic tribe called the Xiongnu[1], who were also known as 'Huns'. (Much later in history they would trouble the Romans too.)

A predecessor of Wudi's had built the Great Wall of China to keep the Huns out; but Wudi had a different plan. He called for a brave official named Zhang Qian (Chang Ch'ien), gave him a hundred men, and sent him west, into the unknown. He hoped that Zhang would pass through Hun territory, find some faraway enemies of the Huns, and make an alliance. Then they could attack the Huns from both sides.

Zhang Qian returned after thirteen years accompanied by only one other survivor from the original company. He brought no good news of military alliances for Emperor Wudi, but he did bring fantastic tales of a new world. He spoke of great cities like Bukhara and Samarkand (both now in Uzbekistan) and the rich Ferghana Valley (now shared between Uzbekistan, Kyrgyzstan and Tajikistan). He had heard intelligence of still more remote kingdoms: Persia, and 'Li-jien' or Rome.

Zhang Qian had discovered the West.

Where explorers lead, exporters follow. Within a hundred years of Zhang Qian's sensational reports, goods were creeping along an arduous network of trade routes between the Chinese and Roman empires. One of the earliest exports from China was an astonishing material, the strongest known natural fabric, light as air and almost see-through: silk. By the time of Christ it had become a must-have fashion material in Rome, despite, or perhaps because of, the disgust of some. (One author wrote how the new silk clothes 'render women naked'.)

Thus, in part because of the demand for designer clothes and exotic fabrics,

Europe and China became trading partners in the last century before Christ. The 'Silk Road' was the link.

A SILKEN THREAD

In ancient times no one travelled the whole length of the Silk Road: goods were bought and sold from trading hub to trading hub along the way. Nor was it a single road: like a packet of data across the Internet, a bundle of silk could travel by a variety of routes through China, Central Asia and Persia before arriving in Damascus or at a Mediterranean port for transhipment to Rome. And much more than silk was traded: other Chinese goodies like furs, ceramics, even rhubarb, hitched a ride west. Travelling the other way were North African gold and other precious metals, ivory, coral, asbestos, and glass.

After the explorers and the exporters came the politics of trade. The desert oasis trading hubs along the route flourished, becoming little kingdoms. Also prospering were Turkic and Tibetan nomadic raiders who preyed on the caravans and on the oasis cities. The Chinese periodically intervened to protect the route, at one time building a western extension to their Great Wall.

In the following centuries, parts of the Silk Road passed through many changes of ownership, many of them Turkic, all the while continuing as a highway between East and West. Christianity certainly travelled down it early. Gospels from approximately AD 500 have been found in Far Eastern trading cities along the Silk Road. An Assyrian missionary started work in China's capital in 635.[2] In the tenth century, Islam followed, carried by nomadic Arabs. In its wake great Islamic civilisations developed, especially in cities like Bukhara which itself became a substantial empire.

MONGOLS AND CHRISTIANS

Starting from 1218, a new, and most deadly, movement of Turkic invaders set out across the short grasslands of Central Asia: the Mongols. With a ferocity honed in centuries of inter-tribal raiding, Genghis Khan and his successors became the arch-destroyers of peoples and property from the Pacific coast to the borders of Poland.

In the respites between the wars, however, the flow of trade and ideas increased along the Silk Road, churned up by the Mongol whirlwind. Gunpowder, paper, and printing, for example, are all Chinese innovations that reached the West in Mongol times.

The great Mongol Khans were tolerant of all faiths and in that climate European Christians were able to travel to the East for the first time. The Venetian writer Marco Polo's 24,000km journey took place between 1275 and 1291. A few years earlier, his uncles had brought a request from the Mongol leader Kublai Khan to the Pope, asking for a hundred missionaries to teach the leading men of the Mongol Empire. This opportunity was missed. But in 1289 the Pope did send the Franciscan friar John of Montecorvino to the Mongol capital, Beijing. John apparently started a church there and had baptised 6000 people by 1305.

Around the same time, Eastern Christians were journeying west. In 1287, a Beijing-born Christian Turk named Mark was welcomed in Rome. When some cardinals queried his theological soundness, Mark replied 'The Holy Apostles … taught us the Gospel, and to what they have delivered us we have clung until the present day.' [3] This same emissary went on to serve Holy Communion to King Edward I of England in Bordeaux: a Turkish Christian cleric from China sharing the Lord's Supper with an English King, back in the 13th century.

THE CHRISTIAN MOVEMENT FAILS

Despite all this contact and influence, the Christian movement in Central Asia became terminally weak during Mongol times. For many reasons:

- The Mongols, after laying waste to large parts of the Muslim world, increasingly became Muslims themselves, and less tolerant of Christians.

- The Church was always rather fragile – it was a movement among the ruling elite rather than the masses; it lacked indigenous Bible translations; it was based in a small network of monasteries rather than a larger network of churches; it was also theologically isolated from much of the rest of Christendom.[4]

- It showed signs of moral weakness and of merging with the majority faiths of the region; it was losing its 'saltiness'.

- The frequent wars and mass destruction, and the massacres of whole populations, gravely weakened the whole region.

The last of the Central Asian conquering Khans, Tamerlane (or Timur Lenk, 'the Lame'), a convinced Muslim, was also the most savage of the conquerors and the most complete destroyer. His conquests began in 1358 and ended at his death in 1405. His destruction of Christian monasteries was particularly decisive. Afterwards, according to historian Stephen Neill:

> *Everything of … Christian civilization [had] been swept away. East and West were more completely separated than they had ever been before; and when travel again became possible, from the Christian point of view everything had to be begun afresh.*[5]

ENTER THE RUSSIANS

A small principality named Moscow was the seed from which the next Central Asian empire grew. In the late 15th century, Mongol rule of the steppes was disintegrating through internal conflict. By playing clever power politics, Moscow was able to exploit these weaknesses and start on its own path to empire.

The centuries of Mongol domination and stagnation had made the Russians determined never again to be invaded from the east. So as Russia grew in power under its great Emperors – Ivan III, Peter, Catherine – it slowly took control of the Central Asian steppes. For four centuries, according to writer Peter Hopkirk, Russia expanded at a steady rate of 20,000 square miles a year.[6] This creeping invasion continued into the late 19th century when Russia took control of what are now the '-stans'. It only halted in 1979 with the failed Soviet invasion of Afghanistan.

UNDER THE COMMUNISTS

Via the Russians the peoples of Central Asia got their first taste of that evolving mass of Western cultural elements that is now called 'globalisation' and that in various forms is so deeply shaking the entire Muslim world.[7] They got a rather strong dose.

It's easy to forget that Communism, in its day, was the most modern, progressive movement around – pro-women, pro-equality, pro-industry, anti-feudal, a tempting solution-in-a-box for economically backward societies. Communism spread schools and hospitals through Central Asia. It led (after many deaths) to increased life expectancies and a decrease in poverty. It turned Central Asia even into a launchpad for space exploration. Communism 'worked' (at least in part and for a time) – but at a brutal price.

- Millions of people were taken out of their traditional nomadic life and herded onto giant state farms or *Kolkhoses*. One researcher wrote: 'During the heyday of the great agricultural collectivisation ... the number of people living in Kazakhstan dropped from 6 to 3 million. From 1929 to February 1932 the number of livestock dropped by more than 85%, from about 40 million to 5.4 million.' Collectivisation led to terror and starvation.

- Religions were persecuted and driven underground. Mosques were closed down.

- Great industrial schemes were attempted and many Russians were brought in to Central Asia to run the factories and hospitals and teach in the schools. Cities were founded.

- Central Asia became the Soviet Union's Cold War scribble pad, the home of freaky science. Kazakhstan hosted over 500 nuclear tests. As a result of these and Chinese tests nearby, children are born today with deformed limbs or no eyes near the testing site of Semipalatinsk.[8] Political prisoners worked the local uranium mines. An island on the Aral Sea was given over to biological warfare research; it's inhabited today by space-suited American scientists trying to shovel the deadly anthrax out of the soil.[9]

- Enormous economic experiments were conducted – not least the idea of turning Uzbekistan and Kazakhstan into a cotton and wheat factory using water from the rivers that fed the Aral Sea. By the time Communism crumbled, the Aral had lost half its original volume and depth, its saltiness had increased three-fold, and most of its fish had died. It may be the world's greatest human-made ecological disaster. Meanwhile, soil erosion has reduced the cotton and wheat crop, and permanently degraded the land.

Still deeper than all this was a damage done to the peoples of Central Asia that many observers notice even if they find it hard to describe exactly. Somehow it seems that the Communist years smothered initiative, optimism, zest, the passion to change the world.

'People say they want to be entrepreneurs but they won't even write a business plan,' one observer and would-be investor told me. Another suggested, 'Perhaps all the people who showed initiative were sent to the labour camps.'[10]

THE RUSSIANS GO HOME

A famous cartoon in the late 1980s showed a rather puzzled God reviewing world history like a video-tape. 'Oops' said the slogan. 'I accidentally pressed FAST FORWARD.'

It seemed a bit like that to many who lived through the domino-like collapse of Communism between 1989 and 1991. What had once been a grey Communist porridge suddenly crystallized into more than a dozen bright new nations. Soviet central planning and control gave way to a freedom so free that it was really economic and political chaos. Dissidents became presidents (though not in Central Asia). Statues of Lenin toppled. Many Russians went home, taking their money and missiles with them, their main fight now their home country's economic disintegration. In a breath, the world changed.

For the states left behind, the loss of Communism was a bit like the sudden death of an abusive parent. Left behind was a complex mix of damage, sorrow, regret – and a rare chance for a new start. Somewhere mixed up in all this was a new opportunity for the Christian gospel.

Former Soviet Union

The fall of Communism led to seven new states in the Caucasus and Central Asia, from left to right on the map, Georgia, Armenia, Azerbaijan, Kazakhstan, Turkmenistan, Uzbekistan, Tajikistan and Kyrgyzstan. Azerbaijan and the '-stans' contain the bulk of the Turkic peoples. Each is named after the majority people of the land – Kazakhstan, then, means 'Kazakh land'.

All the republics are ethnically rather complex, and this mix is constantly changing as ethnic Russians return to Russia and Central Asian peoples re-settle in their homelands. The main peoples – as described by expatriate observers – are:[11]

Azerbaijanis: (20m) live mainly in Azerbaijan and Iran. Originally the Azerbaijanis were fire-worshippers. Later they became Christians for a time, before turning to Islam. They have long known the scars of war in their struggle with Armenia.

Kazakhs (8m): have their home in at least nine Asian countries, with the largest number found in Kazakhstan and northwest China.

Kyrgyz (3m) Like the Kazakhs, the Kyrgyz are traditionally nomads. Shepherds still take their livestock up into the mountains in the summer and live in tents of felt called yurts.

Turkmen (5.4m): are native to northern Afghanistan and Iran, as well as their own republic of Turkmenistan. The president of Turkmenistan calls himself the 'Head of all Turkmen' and his picture can be seen everywhere. Freedom did not last long in Turkmenistan, but the Turkmen Church continues to grow despite the imprisonment, house arrest, and beating of Christian leaders.

Tajiks (4.4m): are also former nomads, and like the Kazakhs and Kyrgyz have been deeply influenced by the Sufi and folk variants of Islam. The Tajiks are unusual in Central Asia in having Persian, rather than Turkic origins.

Uzbeks (20m): Possibly the largest Turkic people group in Central Asia. They have a long history of Islamic influence, and cities in Uzbekistan such as Samarkand and Bukhara were places of renown throughout the Muslim world. Because of this they are more resistant to the gospel than other Turkic people groups. The church has had a slow start, but continues to grow.

China

China has millions of Turkic Muslims, the largest being the 7.4m *Uyghurs*. The Uyghurs live in the beautiful oasis cities around the great deserts of Western China, the Gobi and the Taklamakan. (Taklamakan means something like 'you might go in but you won't come out'.)

Some people have described the Muslim Uyghurs as 'frozen' in the sense that they are locked away within a Communist country with little opportunity to enjoy religious freedoms. They have a strong separatist movement, and are harshly repressed by the Chinese authorities. They hold firmly onto Islam as a way of retaining a national identity.

Uyghur experiences under Chinese Communism have many parallels with their cousins in the former Soviet Central Asia. They have suffered greatly, and been somewhat modernized, under grandiose Communist plans. Islam has been suppressed. Their province has been colonized by the dominant ethnic group (in the Uyghurs' case, the Han Chinese rather than the Russians), and used for nuclear weapons testing. Observers report the same fatalism among the Uyghurs as found among the former Soviet peoples.

Yet by some means or another, Chinese Uyghurs are encountering the gospel and a few have turned to Christ. Many more Uyghurs have turned to Christ across the border in Kazakhstan – though Christians still remain a small minority even here.

Russia

Among the Muslim groups in Russia are the *Tatars* (7m).

Saint Basil's cathedral in Moscow's Red Square is a reminder of Ivan the Terrible's defeat of the Tatars in 1552 and subsequent attempts at forced conversion to Christianity. These attempts were repelled but have left Tatars bruised and wary of Christians. A semi-autonomous republic of Tatarstan exists within Russia today (its capital was a major centre of Islamic learning in the 19th century), but most Tatars live in other parts of Russia and Central Asia.[12] One observer notes: 'There are around 7 million Tatars within the former USSR, at least twice the population of the Kyrgyz and Turkmen. However, since the Tatars do not have their own state, they have been largely overlooked by Christians.'

The *Bashkort* (1m), another group of Turkic Muslims, live in the Russian autonomous province of Bashkortostan, a land of fields and forests the size of France. People turned to Christ in the 1990s from both Tatar and Bashkort communities, not least via work in the local universities.

The *Gagauz* (200,000) have traditionally been Orthodox Christians and were thus quite a rare group among Turkic peoples. Most live in Eastern European countries like Moldova and Romania. Several thousand have come to a living faith in Christ in the last decade.[13]

Russia's most newsworthy Muslim groups are those of the northern Caucasus. The most famous, the *Chechens* (1m), are not a Turkic people. Along with the 600,000 Dagestanis next door, they have lived in their region for as long as their history can be traced.

Chechnya has a long history of rebellion against the Russian state. At the time of writing Chechnya is a warzone. Many refugees, Christians among them, have fled. The grave danger means very little evangelistic activity is possible in Chechnya at the moment.

– 2 –
The Church hatchery

In a book I wrote in 1984,[14] I said that offering the gospel to the Muslim peoples of Albania – 'fenced off by Communism and Islam' – was an example of the impossible tasks that still lay ahead for the Church. I could equally have made the Central Asian peoples of the Communist world my example. They seemed a challenge for another generation.

As late as the 1980s it was all but impossible for a Christian from the free world to travel to Soviet Central Asia. Literature was censored. No usable New Testaments existed in the Central Asian languages. And only a handful of Central Asian Christians were known of.

By the end of the 1990s there were Turkic and Persian churches, evangelical alliances, New Testaments, children's Bibles, Bible schools, Christian-inspired business initiatives. Central Asian Christians from one area were making mission trips to other areas. Looking across the entire Turkic world from Bulgaria to

China, Luis Bush of the *AD2000 and Beyond* networking movement reported 43,000 Turkic evangelicals in 1999.[15] The (Persian) Tajik Christians had increased from approximately zero to 800 in the same period.

How did it happen?

PIONEERS

Some evangelical pioneers served Christ in Central Asia in the 19th and early 20th centuries. Among them:

- George Hunter of the China Inland Mission (now OMF) preached the gospel for fifty-seven years among Central Asian peoples (including thirteen months in a Soviet prison cell). He translated gospels into three Central Asian languages and was awarded an MBE by the British government for his efforts. He died only in 1946, and is buried in the place he made his headquarters, Urumqi in Xinjiang Autonomous Region, in China.[16]

- A Swedish missionary, Niels Fredrick Hoijer, started working among the Uygurs in Xinjiang in 1892. Eventually 60 missionaries served there, translating scripture, and starting churches, orphanages, and clinics. Their work was ended catastrophically with a Muslim uprising in 1938, during which most of the male Uyghur Christians were killed, the females forced to marry Muslims, and the missionaries thrown out at gunpoint.

- Three intrepid middle-aged single women, Mildred Cable, Evangeline French and Francesca French made a pioneering evangelistic trip across Central Asia in the 1920s, becoming the first Western women to cross the Gobi desert. Later they returned to do itinerant evangelism in that same region.[17]

STALIN AND CHURCH GROWTH

Soviet conquest led to many Russians moving to Central Asia. To add to the brew, Stalin then used Central Asia as a safe place to dump millions of 'untrustworthy elements'. During World War II, he deported Germans, Ukrainians, Poles, Bulgarians and Moldavians safely away from the invading German Army. He also pulled Koreans from the east into Central Asia.

Stalin thus posted many evangelicals – Russian and Ukrainian Baptists and Pentecostals, and German Lutherans and Mennonites – into a Central Asia that was lacking evangelical Christian witness. One of the 20th century's great enemies of the Christian faith, he helped start the 21st century Central Asian Church.

None of the Christian groups had a big vision at the time to offer the gospel to the Central Asian peoples. For much of the 20th century they had enough problems holding on to their faith for themselves while their pastors were being shot, their husbands arrested, their Bibles confiscated, their children ridiculed.

And the cultural gulf between these groups and the Central Asian peoples was wide.[18] However, a few Central Asians did bravely join these churches even in Communist times. A few evangelical congregations even made attempts to share the good news about Christ with local people, probably breaking all kinds of laws to do so. They discreetly passed out Russian gospels. A very few even began to think about translating the Bible into the Turkic languages.

MUSTARD SEEDS

At the same time, a little was happening outside the Soviet Union too.

- From the 1970s onward, people began quietly to work on providing New Testaments for the peoples of Soviet Central Asia. Much of this work was pioneered by the Institute for Bible Translation in Sweden.

- In the early 1980s a small number of people around the world began to sense a call from God to serve as Christian workers among the Muslims of Central Asia. This was – even for missionaries – an unfashionable, even slightly mad, idea.

- In Xinjiang, in the 1980s, internally exiled Han Chinese believers began to work on translating scripture portions into Uyghur.

Add up all this quiet activity and even in 1990 it didn't amount to much.

In that year, a networking meeting for all Western mission groups who were interested in the Muslims of Central Asia – the first 'Central Asia Consultation' – attracted just 28 participants. Together, they listed a dozen missions that supposedly wanted to serve in Central Asia. Only half a dozen of these actually were doing anything. The Consultation counted (on their fingers) the Turkic Christians they knew of in Russian or European churches. But they knew of no true Central Asian churches.

AND THE WALLS CAME TUMBLING DOWN

Shock was probably the first impression across Central Asia when Communism imploded, followed by frantic activity. In a few short months five '-stans' were reborn as new nations. So were their cousins across the Caspian Sea, Azerbaijan, Georgia and Armenia. Down at the grassroots, people were losing their jobs (to recession), their pensions and savings (to inflation and devaluation), and their social security (to state bankruptcy). They also lost something else: the package of beliefs about the world and their place in it that had been forced on them for 70 years.

The result – and the story of the 1990s – was of people who were gathered under the Communist 'roof' suddenly finding they had no shelter.

THE CHURCH HATCHERY

After the crash, a number of the more Russified Central Asian people started attending the Russian, German or Korean churches. Some liked what they heard

---

CONFUSED WITHIN

The upheavals of the past years have left many people's beliefs having more in common with a soggy mush than anything anyone (Muslim, Atheist or Christian) would recognise as orthodox belief:

'I know a power observes the world. He is watching and He will punish. This I am sure, but I don't know his name ...'
Gulya, a 21-year old Kazakh, searches for both the name of God and her Kazakh identity.
'Nothing makes sense,' she blurts out. 'I used to be so sure of what I believed. Now I don't know what's true. I want to know. When I was growing up, my mother always told me that to be Kazakh was to be Muslim, yet my family didn't follow the traditions.
'In school I was encouraged to join the young Communist club ... believe in myself ... believe in Communism – just don't believe in God. Communism was something that I believed. It was something that I wanted, but it lied. All lies.
'I never considered believing in God. What could God do for me? I remember shouting cruel names at the one God-believer in my school. Everything about her was different, so we made her life a living hell. Even our school directors treated her badly.
'Now, I just don't know ... there must be something more, something true.' [19]

---

and turned to Christ. (Many others of course stepped up their practice of Islam or made different paths for themselves.)

These little churches became a hatchery for indigenous Central Asian churches. A Russian Christian leader – a man whose great-grandfather was killed under Stalin's purges and whose father was imprisoned for ten years under Brezhnev – explained to me what happened:

1 The numbers of Central Asian believers in Russian and German churches multiplied.

2 They began to realise that they could have their own meetings within the Russian church, in their own languages.

3 Some Russian pastors woke up to what was happening. They started supporting national activity, training leaders.

4 Some of these pastors helped establish new independent churches especially for these converts from a Muslim background.

5 As Russians and Europeans left Central Asia, and Turkic and Persian people turned to Christ, the local element in the Christian scene grew significantly.

Not all the church leaders helped. Some – I was told – looked down on the Muslim background believers in the same way as the Muslim peoples had always been looked down upon within the Soviet Union.

The churches themselves carried scars from their years of isolation and battering. They could be accused of being inward-looking, divided, legalistic, and poor at handling change. But they had stuck out the years of persecution, they were still serving Christ, and they were in the right place at the right time for the peoples of Central Asia.

ENTER THE WORLD

At the same time, from many places in the world, you could almost hear the sound of buckles being fastened and suitcases being zipped as Christian, cultic, Muslim and who-knows-what-else religious workers packed their bags for Central Asia. Central Asia quickly became the destination of choice for short-term volunteers of every religious stripe. If the peoples of Central Asia weren't confused enough already about what to believe, they soon would be.

THE INEXPLICABLE

Then, alongside all the explicable history, some inexplicable history began to happen too.

Bulgaria stands at the far west of the Turkic world. It too, of course, enjoyed a transition from Communism. Bulgarians look down on their Turkish minority. The Turkish minority look down on the Millet, a community who speak a dialect of Turkish and like many similar minorities around the world live lives dogged by unemployment, illiteracy, poor health, alcoholism, domestic violence and family breakdown.

During the early 1990s something happened among the Millet that even those who know them best can't explain too well. One worker described it:

> The Church among them mushroomed after the fall of Communism, probably due to a freeing in the spiritual atmosphere as well as removal of the Communist restrictions on travel. It is estimated that more than ten thousand have become believers [in the 1990s]. This has been a spontaneous people movement to Christ, virtually devoid of outside influence.

The Millet had a Pentecostal awakening. They experienced powerful healings and saw visions and dreams which led them to start worshipping Christ.

Despised and rejected by the majority peoples (Bulgarians and [mainstream] Turks), the Millet are excited and filled with overwhelming gratitude to Jesus when He demonstrates His love for them through miraculous healings and other power encounters.

The Millet are superb evangelists. Everywhere they go they gossip the gospel. On visiting new villages or towns for any reason, they seek out the sick, pray for them, and generally see them healed.

As you might expect, it is also a very unbalanced movement. It includes masses of women and children and very few men. Some of the visions people see are bizarre and disturbing in the extreme. Then, an inability to discern between good and evil leads to legalism.

Though this is a huge challenge to the people from the wider Church who are now involved in teaching the Millet, it shouldn't be a surprise. Awakenings are like this. The churches in the New Testament that sparked off apostolic letters had similar problems.

What *is* surprising is that there is a Church among the Millet at all. No church group started it, no researcher predicted it, it was part of no trend. In a forgotten corner of the 145m-strong Turkic world, God broke down the door and burst in, messily but effectively.

WHATEVER NEXT

That, then, is an outline of what happened among Central Asian people in the 1990s – a movement to Christ that involved local churches, expatriate believers, the collapse of former ideologies, and sovereign and inexplicable acts of God. Days like this do not come around too often.

Next we look at some of the detail, the needs, and the prospects for this surprising Church.

> *Holy places will never be empty.*
> Russian proverb

– 3 –
The surprising Church

You can report on the Central Asian Church in two seemingly opposite ways. Both are true:

- ... like the book of Acts
- ... like the cults

... LIKE THE BOOK OF ACTS

Central Asia has flavours of the book of Acts in the way people responded to the Christian message, the sudden appearance of Christian groups in unexpected places, the large urban churches, the surprising stories, the miracles, the persecutions. Unlike some pioneer situations (Japan springs to mind) where every church is known about and recorded, here in Central Asia there is an uncontrolled, open-ended feel to the story. For example:

- '[Shortly after the fall of Communism] The Chairman of the Baptist Union of Uzbekistan ... discovered a Turkmenian village with thirty inhabitants who were all Christians. It had begun with a Russian soldier who, whilst passing through the village had spoken about Jesus. A little while later a few New Testaments in Turkmen arrived. After the people had read them they all gave their hearts to Jesus.'[20]

- A young woman who had turned to Christ in a city was visited by a former school friend from a rural part of Kazakhstan. The school friend had also turned to Christ. Yet no-one in the city knew of any Christian work in her region.

- One Christian group supplied 300,000 children's Bible storybooks to local schools. In one place, the storybooks were given to the children to take home. In a story-telling culture such as is found in Central Asia, this meant Bible stories were told up and down four generations of families. Months later, a Korean group arrived to show the *Jesus* film – thinking they were the first on the scene – and were very surprised to find families already familiar with the stories of Christ.

It isn't unusual to find a handful of churches in a typical Central Asian city. One might be a cell-church planted out from a large congregation in the capital. Another may have started around the Christian witness of expatriate university lecturers. An indigenous Pentecostal group may have started a third. There may be a Korean Pentecostal church or two and perhaps a Russian or German Baptist church. In each case, most of the growth is from Central Asian people experiencing God's love for themselves and inviting in their families and friends.

... LIKE THE CULTS

At the same time, you can also see the evangelicals being given a place in society on the religious fringe, much like the cults.

Protestant Christianity is slightly better established than the cults because Russian or German Protestants have been here for generations, and because Protestantism is a bit more respectable in the world. But for all their recent growth, the tens of thousands of evangelicals in Central Asia still are part of the religious asteroid belt. They are not one of the major planets.

The religious authorities – Muslim and Orthodox Christian – are keen to keep it that way. They like to teach that evangelicals 'give out Bibles and dollars freely'. They say that such activity will only 'inoculate' the people against the 'true faith'. They have encouraged governments to make up laws that will keep out the latest arrivals on the religious scene.

A YOUNG CHURCH

Both descriptions – Book of Acts; irritating minor cult – carry some truth. Possibly the Christianity-as-minor-cult picture is becoming more appropriate as the chaos of the first decade settles down.

This is a young Church, almost a youth movement. Congregations are mostly made up of teenagers or people in their 20s. You can see two main types of young people in these congregations:

1 Poor, largely unemployed, traditional village people who have moved to the city.

2 More highly educated – and thus Russified – students in those same cities.

Understanding this helps us to see the Church's weaknesses, its marginal nature – and its potential. Central Asia's new Christians are characterised by:

Powerlessness: Mostly, it is not village or urban leaders who are coming to Christ. It is the marginalised young people. They can only live out the Christian life with the permission of others. For example, family duties often keep people away from Christian meetings. In a Central Asian family a teenage girl has to help out whenever guests arrive. Sometimes she has to stay at home just in case guests turn up. Other people work long hours to earn enough to live. Such people are what the Church is made of: this adds to the Church's marginal feel.

Volatility: Many people drop away after showing an initial interest in Christian things. This has a striking resonance with Jesus' own time. Chapter 6 of John's gospel, for example, describes many who followed Christ the Miracle Worker turning their back on Christ the Disciple Maker.

Change: Teenagers move on, perhaps to the bigger cities, which means that town churches often struggle with continually re-founding themselves. I know of one church in Azerbaijan, for example, that had baptized perhaps 300 people but that only counted 20 to 30 at its regular meetings. Some had stopped coming, some had to stay at home, some had moved on to study in the capital.

Vulnerability: Many of the converts come from difficult backgrounds, a fact which greatly affects church life. One day some of these people will be mature, godly leaders. Some of them, wonderfully, already are. But others … the head-lines that appear in our Christian magazines and newspapers about 'persecution' in Central Asia are often more accurately about local Christian immaturity. '20-year-old pastor' is often another way of spelling 'trouble'.

In danger over money issues. The implied claim of the religious authorities –

SIGNS AND WONDERS

Signs, wonders and miracles feature large in the Central Asian story. For example, I have heard two or three stories from fairly reliable sources of small-town imams coming to Christ. I wasn't able to check these stories firsthand.[21] They have probably improved in the telling. But such stories are a universal currency in Central Asia; all the front-line workers I spoke to could probably quote one or two.

The village imam is the Muslim leader in the local mosque. But this is a long way from Mecca. As well as leading the standard prayers, he generally acts as faith healer and spirit-expert for the village, manufacturing charms and protective hardware; attempting traditional, and sometimes occult, healing; giving spiritual advice.

In one story I heard, an imam sent two sons to Tashkent to bring back another spiritual healer to cure a grandson. On the bus, these two young men met a Christian who persuaded them to turn round, return home, and let him pray for the grandson instead. They did so. Through prayer to Christ the son was wonderfully healed.

The other sons were impressed enough to turn to Christ for themselves, against the wishes of their father, who threw them all out of the house. But that night, the father had a dream that frightened him deeply. Worse, when he woke up, he found he was blind.

Like the apostle Paul, this imam received his sight back as part of his turning to Christ. He began preaching that Christ was Lord. This split the mosque in two rather in the way that Christian preaching in the first century was splitting synagogues.

What will have happened to that new church since? All the excitement may have died away, leaving a group of untaught semi-believers, who know Power but not Truth. Many in the congregation may never have actually left their folk beliefs and whatever Christian life there is may slowly wither away.

Or, the new Christian group may be making contact with Christians elsewhere who can strengthen them with good teaching, and gradually enfold them in the ongoing life of the wider Church. Either scenario is possible, given Central Asia's vastness.

that the 'conversions to Christ' are primarily for material reasons – is a convenient and credible one. But it is not finally true.

Foreign Christians in Central Asia do meet people every day who want money, jobs, or visas rather more than they want peace with God. It is always difficult to discern between 'true' seekers and time-wasters. Actually, it's impossible, since no single person falls exactly into either category, and since God in his grace can get hold of someone looking for a freebie and turn them into a devoted disciple.

However, I have yet to meet a cross-cultural Christian worker who views with anything other than horror the idea of bribing people into the Kingdom. And in Central Asia any would-be disciple soon has to face not material gain but continuing material need, and then rejection, trouble, even persecution. People who stick with the Christian faith under those circumstances are doing so presumably because they have found that Christ is not so much meal ticket as Bread of Life.

Money issues remain a hazard to the young Church, though. Plenty of Non-Governmental Organizations (NGOs) buzz around the Central Asian Church, eager to help but also creating a hazard.

Take for example a Kazakh young person in a local church who is approached by a rich NGO from overseas. The NGO is looking to have a representative in the region. The young person may speak English and Kazakh and profess faith in Christ, but may otherwise be completely unready for the enormous power that access to outside funds brings. Local pastors bewail this insensitive Christian head-hunting. Unchecked, this kind of thing will give the Church a bad name and destroy lives.

LOOKING GOOD FOR THE FUTURE

The Church, then, has far to go.

The challenge for the Christians is to carve out an identity which is Turkic or Persian (not Russian or Western); wide-hearted (not cultic or sectarian); and worthy of respect (the kind of thing that esteemed family members believe, not just the dropouts). Instead of being few, young, poor, and marginal, the Church has a call to become many, mature and mainstream.

It looks like it is going to be slow work from here. One experienced observer described 'incredible openness' in 1992 but now talks of the 'months and years of prayer, love, and sharing the gospel that are required to win people who are gradually becoming less and less open to the gospel and more focused on traditional spiritual practices or simply putting food on the table.' [22]

Once again, Central Asia at the moment has strong resonances with New Testament times. There, too, the churches were creatures of the margins – household meetings of slaves, former gay temple prostitutes and crooks, for example – with 'not many' pillars of the community holding everything together. Yet these little churches went on, over a few centuries, to become the central, enduring feature of European civilisation. That lofty vision is an (eventual) possibility for the Church in Central Asia, though perhaps none of us will live to see it.

CLEARING A SPACE

What we are seeing already, however, is the Christians clearing a space within the culture for themselves, and slowly becoming distinctive as something more than youth fad or religious cult. This can be seen in a number of ways.

Church growth: Force of numbers is beginning to count. Some of the Central Asian capital cities have churches now with hundreds of members. Turkmenistan, despite close government control, may now have more Central Asian than Russian believers. Alliances are being formed between Central Asian church groups.

It's easy to overstate this. Very many Christians in Central Asia, outside the few large city congregations, feel isolated and alone. The Central Asian Church is only big when you compare it with other Muslim-background churches around the world. But it is big enough to have a certain viability and visibility.

Working with culture: What to do with the bread that is baked in many Central Asian homes as a way of celebrating and appeasing the Ancestors? Should Christian homes bake it? Who will bury me when I die? How should weddings and births be celebrated in ways that pay respect both to tradition and to Christian teaching? These things are being actively discussed by church groups across Central Asia. Distinctively Central Asian, distinctively Christian families and households are being created. These people are re-writing their culture according to a Christian script.

Creativity: Indigenous Christian art and music is being created. This art is something quite new in the culture: authentic, local, fresh, distinctively Christian.

Nation building: Local Christians, often in partnership with outsiders, are creating local charities to work in areas like agriculture and commerce; vocational training; rehabilitation for drug and alcohol addicts.

A TINY CHURCH

We can conclude, then, that the church in Central Asia is at the moment:

- Only a tiny part of the overall scene

- Sociologically part of the religious fringe

- Made up of teenagers who may grow out of all this

And yet... mission history is a continual retelling of the Parable of the Mustard Seed: the tiny speck becomes the tree where the birds roost. No-one knows if the

current tiny speck of the Church will this time grow into something that offers shade to all the sunny plains of Central Asia. Central Asia has, after all, been unsuccessfully evangelized several times before in history.

If it happens at all, it will surely be when through God's power the Church demonstrates an integrity and a comprehensiveness beyond the simple gathering of converts. Such growth has happened before, all over the world and in many diverse cultures. How may it happen in Central Asia? What are the specific challenges? The next chapter investigates.

THE POWER OF PARTNERSHIP

When a disaster happens, or a new opportunity for ministry suddenly opens up, conventional wisdom expects one of two responses from the evangelical groups:

1 They miss it completely, or arrive on the scene too late, with too little.

2 There is an uncoordinated 'feeding frenzy' of Non-Governmental Organizations – including the evangelical agencies and church groups. In the worst case NGOs fight turf wars, race to hire local community leaders, and send out journalists and photographers to produce good fund-raising copy. In the words of an Indian writer, 'Everyone loves a good famine.'

Neither happened among the Christians when Central Asia suddenly opened in 1991. Instead, what happened between 1990 and 2000 was one of the best examples I have ever seen of creative networking between evangelical organisations.

This partnership started with the first 'Central Asia Consultation' in 1990 – a meeting of Bible smugglers, translators, pioneer missionaries, and people who encouraged the Church in the Communist world. Though at first suspicious of each other (these were secretive and dangerous days), they agreed to meet annually. Slowly, the barriers came down and true networking began. Smaller, special-interest partnerships were set up. Some of these focussed on a people (the Kazakhs, say); others on a major issue (for example, Business Development).

The annual Central Asia Consultation and its smaller specialist partnerships grew rapidly through the early 1990s as first dozens, then hundreds, of mission agencies and church groups got involved. It has not been without its setbacks, failures, and weaknesses. But the Consultation quickly became the essential first stop for any evangelical group that wants to serve in Central Asia. Want to meet, for example, the more than 70 agencies from 20 nations who are seeking to serve in Kazakhstan or among Kazakhs? You can, by contacting the Kazakh Partnership. Want to serve Christ by – say – selling Central Asian crafts in the West? Try the Central Asian Business Consultation.

– 4 –
The road ahead

Two immediate challenges stand out for the Church as it tries to spread a flavour of Christ throughout Central Asia.[23]

They are:

- Thriving in an Islamic context

- Being relevant in the economic context.

ISLAM MY HOME

Take Islam first. Islam will still set the faith context for Central Asia for the foreseeable future. Most Turkic Central Asians will likely call themselves Muslims at the end of 21st century, as at the beginning (barring some theological earthquake).

Central Asian Islam is a little like a thin, battered tin can that safely holds together a community that is mostly characterised by mushy, unIslamic beliefs:

- *Thin:* Central Asia's Muslims subscribe to a moderate school of Islam. Maybe only a third do the daily prayers. Half the population may observe Ramadan but for three days rather than the full month.[24] It's quite rare ever to hear the call to prayer. Women's dress codes are relaxed.

- *Battered:* Islam had to survive the forced conversions to atheism of the Communist years. The Muslim community, not less than the Christian one, has its martyrs and heroes and stories of courage.

- *Tough:* There's a steely strength to this container. Central Asia's Islam is part of a heritage of social and family ties and festivals that, taken as a package, the peoples of Central Asia deeply love and hold on to tenaciously. This is home for them.

- *Strange contents:* Central Asian Islam is a surprise, though, to people familiar with other parts of the Muslim world, such as South Asia or the Arab World. It's a religious vacuum. What rush to fill the vacuum are superstition and total confusion. The obsession with superstition is something that Central Asia shares with the whole Islamic world (and with many other places). The confusion, it shares with other regions whose faith-edge has been dulled by generations of materialism, such as the post-Christian West. Jesus is wonderful, Central Asian Muslims will tell you. Marvellous. We'll believe in him – as well as in the old traditions, in reincarnation, UFOs, and the healing power of crystals and pyramids. I think Buddhism has a lot to teach us as well. And I'll have my palm read. Everything leads to God after all, even things that are utterly irreconcilable and contradictory.

The Church will have to live and think carefully if it is to thrive in this setting. Islam forms the backdrop; confusion and superstition are people's daily experience. Somehow, the Church will have to demonstrate that following Jesus works better than all this, personally and culturally.

FEAR OF REVOLUTION

The second issue with the Islamic context of Central Asia is that governments fear it. They have some reason to. Islam offers one of the few available rallying points if you want to upset the political order. Many of the Muslim workers who have entered Central Asia have just that agenda.

Muslim activities have led to some furious backpedalling on religious freedom in the '-stans'. Police tactics from Communist days have reappeared. The squeeze on religious activity affects everyone, Muslims, Christians and cults.

Leading the way is Uzbekistan (with Turkmenistan close behind). Uzbeks have always taken their Islam rather more seriously than the nomadic Kazakhs, Tajiks, Turkmen, and Kyrgyz peoples. (The outstanding Islamic architecture of some Uzbek cities is silent testimony of that.) The Ferghana Valley, shared between several Central Asian states, has been home to Central Asia's scariest examples of political Islam. Muslim workers have made nearby Tashkent, the Uzbek capital, their centre of operations for the re-Islamizing of Central Asia. Muslim revolutionaries are not popular with the people, even in the Ferghana Valley. But they scare dictators.

The return of Soviet-style repression in Uzbekistan has also squeezed the Church. Ordinary Uzbeks are at the time of writing handing back Bibles, books and tapes lent them by their Christian friends. Fear is in the air. Pastors have been arrested on what appear to be faked charges of drug possession. Church meetings are raided. Uzbekistan recently was ranked one of the ten worst countries on the planet for religious freedom.[25]

After a few short years of freedom, the young Uzbek Church seems to be being pitched into a season of trials and 'patient endurance' which is a great challenge.

BUILDING THE NATION

Now the economic context. Imagine the inflation of the 1970s, the high unemployment and deep recessions of the 1980s, and the globalizing pressures of the 1990s. Make them more intense than they ever were in the West. Make them all happen at once. And you have a flavour of what is happening in the former Soviet Union.

The region's economies broke up. Hyperinflation appeared. The factories, hospitals and schools, in the harsh light of world standards, suddenly looked decrepit. And then, with the breakup of the Soviet Union (or the 'peeling of the Soviet Onion' as someone called it) old patterns of trade completely unravelled.

One example: a clothing factory in Kazakhstan was used to receiving textiles from Latvia and then selling its finished goods to the state trading company which supplied Soviet shops. Without state-subsidised transport, the cloth from Latvia became too expensive. Without money, the state trading company didn't want the clothes. Hyperinflation was raging around the stranded factory and they had no cash to pay their workers. Nor could they upgrade their factory to world standards or develop new markets. Their managers, economists and financial planners had not been trained for all this. How could they not go bankrupt?

Watch the factories and the state farms imploding one by one and you have a clue to the defining, daily problem in Central Asia today. Large parts of the economy have died. The surviving parts are disconnected from each other. The Russians who built the system have left. What was once a simple Soviet industrial scene is now a thousand-piece jigsaw, with most of the pieces missing.

GIVE US OUR DAILY BREAD

Poverty and uncertainty is the result.

No longer, in Central Asia, will a couple come home from a week at work with pay-packets that will buy the groceries. No longer can people rely on free education or health care, or subsidised transport. What happens when the pillars that support modern life crumble? Come to Central Asia and find out: electricity, water, heating, health care, education, wages become unreliable and intermittent. Your back yard becomes more important as a source of food than your university degree. Urbanites have to learn how to be peasants. Farmers' fields languish for lack of machinery. Pensioners and invalided war heroes sell single cabbages or shoelaces or their own possessions on the streets.

STILL GRIEVING

Across Central Asia people still grieve the loss of the Soviet Union. They were part of a superpower – now they belong to a small, poor country. For a generation, they were taught they lived in Utopia: now, the state that provided for them has died. Most people in Central Asia will tell you 'It was better back then.' The Soviet Union may have been an abusive parent, but it was still a parent.

EVERY FAMILY FOR ITSELF

What takes the place of the old certainties? A fight for survival, sadly by unfair means as well as by fair ones.

- One way of coping is *taking bribes*. The dire economic needs have tempted every state official, small and great, to supplement their shrunken wages with bribes.

- Another way of coping is *fantasising*. The president of Turkmenistan has built a string of 25 Western-style hotels in the Karakum desert. They are mostly empty. 'We will build hotels, and the world will come to us,' he argued. He is an extreme example. But his actions are a sign that the former Soviet world is vulnerable to all kinds of get-rich-quick schemes.

- Some have found jobs in the *few foreign companies* that have managed to set up and make money within the bureaucratic jungle that is Central Asia.

- Almost everyone tries to *grow their own food*. Some will even keep a cow or two if the small plot of land around their house permits it.

- And of course many of the *old jobs* have survived, though without paying nearly so well. Many people work a couple of hours each day at the factory, before heading off to try to make real money at a second job.

- Many people have set up *small businesses*. Among them are taxi-services, small restaurants, hairdressers. Most popular is what is often called 'suitcase trading': buying something in one area to sell in another. Suitcase traders have been known to charter buses to China, or planes to Turkey. Leaving home with a wad of dollars from previous trades, they return with plastics or clothes to sell in local markets.

THE CALL TO THE CHURCH

It may be that the economic decline of the region has finally halted. But it should be no surprise that high up on the list of needs in Central Asia are sound, solid, honest business investments. The cry I heard from both local and expatriate Christians is for help with building businesses in this new world.

This is at least as urgent as the more obvious priority of investing in the internal workings of the Church itself.

WHY THE CHURCH?

Why should the church get involved? Many reasons.

- Hope. In Central Asia there is a shortage of hope. Even by small acts the Church challenges the prevailing gloom.

- Unemployment. In Kazakhstan, for example, un- and under-employment taken together is somewhere between 40 and 60%. One foreign businessman said this: 'Jesus refers to ways we can help our neighbours: "I was hungry and you fed me, I was thirsty and you gave me a drink" and so on. I believe we could add, "I was unemployed and you gave me a job." '[26]

- Historically the Church around the world has always fitted in where the practical needs are most acute: sometimes bringing health care, sometimes education, sometimes disaster relief. In Central Asia the pressing need is to rebuild economies and societies.

- *Christian* businesses are needed especially in these societies because (theoretically) they will bring with them commitments to financial integrity, long-termism, investing in people, and caring for the environment.

- Investing in Central Asia will demonstrate that the evangelical church is not simply into rounding up herds of converts, but genuinely committed to incarnating Christ within the cultures of Central Asia; this is how we love our neighbours.

- Building sound businesses of integrity does have the side-effect of creating sound families and helping local people create healthy churches.

Some Christian business people are catching onto the vision. One small group of expatriates set a goal of helping create 60–80 new businesses in Kazakhstan

---

BUSINESS VENTURES

Potential business ventures come in all shapes and sizes. Here's a sample of what some of the Christians have been getting up to:

- An urban family bought an ice-cream-cone maker in one Central Asian country. By putting in long hours of work, and going into a lot of debt, they eventually started pulling their family finances back into shape again.

- A group in one area started a business making tombstones. As well as providing an income, it made a statement about overcoming the fear of death.

- Someone hand-sews fur hats, a good business in a country where temperatures can sink to an invigorating −45 C. With relatively small investment (a sewing machine) he could increase his production dramatically from the current four or five hats per day.

- Another family bought and overhauled an old butter packaging machine. Successful with this, they now want to add other food packaging lines to their business.

- One group, with expatriate help, are working to create specialist travel firms offering mountain-climbing tours to previously inaccessible peaks.

- One person is producing Mozzarella cheese using local ingredients as a replacement for the more expensive imported variety.

- Some are setting up print and copy shops.

- A dairy farmer is trying to add value to his business by buying bottling equipment.

All these businesses could bloom given a few nuggets of help: some capital, some consultancy, some training. Potentially, thousands of business people in developed countries could serve Christ through partnerships with these businesses and entrepreneurs. Several networks already exist that will function as 'marriage bureaux' for such partnerships (see the resources section).

---

before 2002. Working in partnership with expatriates already in the country, they are identifying local entrepreneurs and offering training, consultancy, and help with finding capital and markets.

The range of opportunities for Christian service are huge. For example:

- Part of the way to help integrate Central Asia into world markets is by teaching English. Central Asia has room for thousands of volunteer English teachers. So, incidentally, has Xinjiang province of China.

- Business professionals and trainers are needed to speak in business colleges.

- Expatriate entrepreneurs are needed to help create businesses.

- Investors are needed to supply micro-credit, and bigger loans, and perhaps to include consultancy and partnership with their loan.

- Christians are sorely needed to work within multinationals in private business and fulfilling government contracts.

SUMMARY

To conclude:

- The 1990s was an era of loss in Central Asia. The Soviet Union died. Nothing has yet replaced it.

- In the midst of this, a Church has sprung up.

- The Church has the opportunity to become a vital part of whatever new cultures evolve. But it is young, and small, and on the fringes. It may seize the opportunity or – through persecution perhaps, or by falling at any of the many hurdles ahead – squander it and not have a similar opportunity again for many years.

Next we look at Turkey, a nation where a fragile church has also come into being, but by a much different route.

Turkey

CHRISTIAN TURKEY

Wind the video back to the first 300 years of Christian history, and what is now Turkey dominates the story.

Tarsus in Cilicia, Paul's home, is located in modern-day Turkey. So is Antioch (called Syrian Antioch in the Bible but actually modern Antakya in S E Turkey). This Antioch church saw Christians first called 'Christians', experienced the first flowering of the gospel among the Gentiles, and sent out a rather distinguished list of missionaries: Paul, Barnabas, Mark and Silas. Much of the New Testament was first written for churches in what is now Turkey.[27] The church in Ephesus, in Turkey, counted Paul, Timothy and John among its first few leaders – not a bad start.

The Church was still thriving after the era of the first apostles ended. Early in the second century AD, Pliny the Younger (incidentally, the same Roman official

who objected to women wearing silk) governed in Turkey. He reported to the Roman Emperor how in his province 'many of every age, every class and of both sexes' were thought to be Christians. Pagan temples had become 'well-nigh abandoned'.[28] Pliny was trying – and failing – to stop the rot.

Two hundred and fifty years further on, the Emperor Julian complained about the Christians' 'benevolence to strangers – their care for the graves of the dead, and the apparent holiness of their lives.' The Christians, he complained, 'support not only their own poor but ours as well.'[29] In due time Turkey became the heart of the Christian-in-name Byzantine Empire, with Constantinople (now Istanbul) its capital.

NO WONDER THE CHURCH GREW

Turkey had its share of early Christian martyrs. In 156AD, the church leader in Smyrna (modern Izmir), an 86-year-old named Polycarp was arrested. In his youth he had known the apostle John and was the last link with the people who saw Christ in the flesh. The charge, as ever, was refusal to say 'Caesar is Lord.' He had the following conversation with the Proconsul of Asia, before he was burnt alive at the stake:

Proconsul: 'Have respect for your age. Swear by the divinity of Caesar; repent and say, "Away with the atheists".'

Polycarp: (signalling towards the largely pagan crowd): 'Away with the atheists!'

Proconsul: 'Take the oath, and I will let you go; revile Christ.'

Polycarp: 'Eighty-six years have I served Him, and He has done me no wrong; how then can I blaspheme my Saviour and King?'[30]

BYZANTINE COMPLICATIONS

How the Church fell from all that power and influence need not detain us. But about a thousand years ago, Muslim Turkic nomads began conquering modern Turkey. In 1134 a Turkic dynasty, the Seljuks, made Konya – Iconium of the book of Acts – their capital city, and inaugurated a wonderful flowering of urban civilisation and fine architecture.

A century later came the Mongol conquests under Genghis Khan. Turkic war-lords, forced westward, conquered yet more of modern Turkey and gradually gained power over the weakening Seljuks. A warlord named Osman eventually became the dominant male and founded a dynasty that lasted until modern times – the Ottomans.

The Ottomans famously conquered Constantinople in 1453 and continued to expand into Europe and Russia up to the 17th century. Folk memories from Ottoman times still colour European, Turkish, Christian and Muslim attitudes today:

- For the Europeans in the 17th century the Ottoman Empire was the 'present terror of the world'[31], and the propaganda of the day made much of its cruelty, immorality, and despotism. Later, as the Empire began to degenerate, and European power grew, it became the 'sick man of Europe', a debtor nation, dangerously unstable, savagely turning on its Christian minorities, finally put to death in the trauma of World War I.

- From a Turkish and Muslim perspective, however, the Ottoman Empire was a breath of clean air sweeping away the corruption and poison of the Byzantine Empire. This pure Muslim empire was then undermined from without by the scheming and immoral European Christians, and from within by secessionist Christian communities.

The equating of 'Christian' with 'Europe' and 'Muslim' with 'Turk' and a bloody, complicated history with much unrighteousness and offended pride on all sides is a massive complicating factor for the gospel in Turkey today.

MISSIONS TO TURKEY

Despite these centuries of unpromising context, a few hardy souls have attempted missions to the Ottoman Empire and to Turkey. Back in the mid-16th century a Protestant officer in an army that fought the Ottomans, Freiherr Von Sonegg, spent his whole fortune on producing Christian books for the peoples of the Ottoman Empire. In the early 18th century, the Moravian Church, that most ardently missionary of Protestant denominations, sent workers.

Large scale missions had to wait until the Great Missionary Awakening (1790s onwards). In 1820, the American Mission Board sent two researchers to the Ottoman Empire. Their report led to the first serious, major Protestant missions to what is now Turkey. These early missions saw a little fruit. Some individuals turned to Christ. Small groups of converts did appear, but were snuffed out by persecution.

The existing Christian communities, however, were receptive to the missionaries' message. This was not planned, but it is hard for zealous Christian workers to ignore spiritual hunger pangs. The result was that Protestant missions both revitalised, and split, the ancient Christian communities. At times the split was bitter. The Armenian Patriarch in 1844 expressed the wish that evangelicals would be buried so deep that even the Last Trump would not raise them.[32]

THE DEFINING MOMENT

The death-throes of the Ottoman Empire at the turn of the 20th century were horrible times for the Christian community. The Armenian people – usually on the pretext that they were betraying the state – were massacred in 1895–1896, 1909, and 1915–1916. Well over a million are thought to have lost their lives. Virtually all the Armenians were officially Christians: many probably had a living faith.[33]

At the end of the First World War, Turkey was set to be carved up between the victorious allies. But then Mustapha Kemal Ataturk, the 'Father of the Turks' stepped onto the stage. A hero from Gallipoli, he united the Turks, got rid of the invading allies, and founded modern-day Turkey out of the Ottoman ashes. The nation today still bears his stamp.

First, and famously, Ataturk turned Turkey decisively away from the old ways. He called Islam 'a heavy blanket that keeps the people of Turkey asleep'.[34] He banned the fez, the rimless hat that symbolized a Muslim's willingness to prostrate himself before God. He introduced the Roman alphabet and taught women to read. He made Turkey officially a secular nation and the army the guardian of its secular status.

Second, less famously, he established ethnic Turkishness as the defining element in belonging to Turkey. 'Happy is the man who calls himself a Turk' is painted in army bases and engraved on hillsides.

The problem with ethnic Turkishness as a basis for nationhood, however, is how happy you are if you don't call yourself a Turk.

ONE PEOPLE, ONE NATION

At the beginning of the twentieth century Turkey was perhaps 30% Christian and was a pick-and-mix bag of Turks, Kurds, Armenians, Greeks, Syrians and many others. Nowadays it is officially 85% Turk and 98% Muslim. What happened?

Some of the non-Turks moved away. A million and a half Greeks left Turkey in 1923, for example, and were replaced by almost the same number of Turks from Greece.

Others were killed. For example, in Izmir (Smyrna) perhaps 100,000 people died when Ataturk's army fell upon the refugee-filled city in September 1922.

The ones who didn't leave and weren't killed were 'assimilated'.

'Assimilating' the minorities has involved all the brutality of forcing round pegs into square holes:

- For decades, the Kurds, who make up something between 18% and 25% of the Turkish population were called 'mountain Turks' and were forbidden to use their own language outside of their homes and communities. This oppression led directly to a Kurdish independence movement, which in turn led to a spiral of evil and civil conflict.

- Something like 25% of Turkey's Muslims may be Alevis, belonging to a branch of Shi'a, rather than Sunni, Islam. Alevis are much more keen on seeing a liberal, plural, secular Turkey. They prefer their variant of Islam and

see it as a necessary counterbalance to what they see as legalistic, Arab-inspired Sunni Islam. For years the Alevis have complained of discrimination from the Sunni majority.[35]

- The final glowing embers of the traditional church are being slowly put out, despite the constitutional guarantees of freedom.

- While the openly Armenian community is small, old and declining, close observers of the scene come across many 'Turks' who in unguarded moments will admit to speaking Greek or Armenian in their villages. Officially they are Turks, and Muslims: unofficially, they are part of a large, anonymous community that is keeping its head firmly down.

A BETTER FUTURE?

Life for minorities in Turkey is changing for the better. The Kurds, for example, now have some limited opportunities to use their own language in the mass media. The Alevis are more openly fighting for their rights. Some members of the national assembly are openly Kurdish or Alevi or both.

TURKEY'S CHURCH

What of the church in Turkey? The story of the past 40 years is of a community very slowly re-establishing space for itself in the Turkish context. Years of 20th-century neglect of Turkey by the evangelical wing of the Church came to an end in the early 1960s:

1 Teams of young Christians began entering Turkey on tourist visas, offering gospels to people on the street and holding evangelistic meetings.

2 Other foreign Christians began learning Turkish and taking ordinary jobs in Turkey with the aim of providing a quieter, longer-term testimony to the gospel.

3 Gospel radio broadcasts were begun. Films, books, audio tapes and TV programmes were created. Fresh Bible translations were begun to replace the old Turkish Bible which had become hard to understand. Some people began writing letters almost at random to addresses in Turkey, offering information about the Christian faith. Others placed adverts in Turkish magazines and newspapers. This was all a bit hit-or-miss, but nevertheless generated significant responses.

FIRSTFRUITS

What have been the results? Once again, people from the traditional Christian communities have been coming to a fresh personal faith for themselves.

The other consequence has been the emergence, just about, of a Turkish Church made up of people who started life in the Turkish Muslim communities. This is a first for Turkey, yet it also fits the wider pattern of people from Central Asian Muslim communities turning to Christ.

This church is definitely growing – but you have to look over the perspective of a decade or two, rather than a year or two:

- In the 1960s, Christian researchers knew of only a handful of believers in Christ from a Muslim background in Turkey. Now it is possible to count perhaps 1000 Christians from a Muslim background. You would find a rather smaller number than that actually in church on Sundays; even so, the

Turkish Church is in its way one of the wonders of the Christian world – a testament to faith and tenacity in most difficult circumstances.

- The number of congregations has increased, especially in the 1990s.

- These little churches have suffered a lot. Christians have been repeatedly arrested and beaten. For many years, churches were denied permits to meet. Post Office boxes were raided. Special lists were kept by the military of Christian conscripts to the army. Yet, the Christians' claims that they are not breaking the law has been tested many times in court and proven right each time. So now, thanks to a tough little Church, and thanks to some courageous Muslim judges and lawyers, it is becoming legitimate to be a Christian from a Muslim background, to worship in a church building, and to seek to share one's faith.

- Interest in the gospel has increased, albeit from a very low level. If you tried to give away New Testaments ten years ago, almost no-one you met would touch them. Nowadays, most people will at least accept gospels when offered. In 1999, a group of local churches invited the evangelist Luis Palau to conduct some evangelistic meetings. This mission didn't go entirely to plan (they had a bomb scare, for example) but it was another example of Christians 'coming out' and doing something that a decade ago would have been unthinkable.

A LONG WAY TO GO

Veteran workers to Turkey are amazed by the changes over the last twenty years. They have not seen anything like it in their ministry lifetimes. But there is still a long way to go. Consider:

- The Church is still tiny.

- Many are passing through the Church rather than belonging to it.

- Many are people who were already outcasts from Turkish society, an ex-drug addict here, a former terrorist there. Nothing wrong with this – Jesus came to heal the broken, after all – but it means there are few normal, stable, Christian families and households in the Turkish Church.

- The Church and expatriate Christians are still regularly picked on and thumped by the police and the media. This has happened before: in

Polycarp's time, Christians in Turkey were accused of cannibalism; in the 21st century, media reports tend to accuse Christians of forcing minors to convert or of offering bribes.

- Spiritual conflict is real. Many expatriates, who love Turks and Turkey and who choose to spend their lives in the country, nevertheless testify that the country feels like a 'dark' and oppressive place to live and worship. Some link this perceived darkness with the massacres a century ago, and the fact that the Turkish nation still officially denies they ever happened.[36] Also, the Church suffers seemingly unnatural setbacks. For example, one Turkish city lost two of its key young Christian leaders to sudden death within a short time of each other. One was shot in a random terrorist killing; the second died of a heart attack. Other little congregations have been plagued by sectarianism and betrayal.

THE CHURCH'S DEBT

If the worldwide Church, like that famous son of Turkey, the apostle Paul, is a 'debtor' to the non-Christian world, how can we pay our debt of love to Turkey?[37] We can take a personal part in building the Turkish Church by serving there. While mature, apostolic types are requested by the young Turkish Church, ordinary people may also apply. One observer wrote:

The big need is for very ordinary people who will simply love and share in an outgoing friendly way with their Turkish friends in the course of their daily lives. Those who have come to live in Turkey in this way for any length of time have come to hold a deep affection for the land and its peoples.[38]

We can apply concerted repentance, prayer, and living faith. The recent 'reconciliation walks' of Christians eager to apologize for Christian wrongdoing in Turkey and elsewhere have probably had some effect at some level. The need for ongoing prayer, and for a never-say-die faith – a faith that is more stubborn, and more unyielding than all the problems the Church faces – remains.

THE KURDS

The Kurds are Turkey's largest ethnic minority. (The Alevis are a religious minority, made up both of Kurds and Turks.)

The traditional Kurdish homeland is the mountainous region that connects Turkey, Armenia, Iran, Iraq and Syria – a landscape that contains, among other things, the source of the Tigris and Euphrates rivers, Mount Ararat, and lots of oil.

Kurds sprang to recent international prominence in 1988, when Saddam Hussein killed over 200 of his Kurdish citizens with poison gas, and again in 1991 when Iraqi Kurds rebelled, leading to further attacks by the Iraqi army, a refugee crisis, and the founding of the UN 'safe haven' for Kurds. The 'safe haven' in Northern Iraq is the first time Kurds have had a homeland to call their own for many centuries.

Virtually all the Kurdish minorities have tried to break away from their host nation at some point in the twentieth century; Turkey's Kurdish Workers' Party movement has been the most violent.

The Kurds understand themselves to be the descendants of the Medes of old. If that's so – and there's no other coherent body of people from the same region with the claim – they can count such Biblical luminaries as Darius the Mede as their ancestor. Some of the Israelites from the Northern Kingdom were exiled 'in the towns of the Medes', never to return.[39]

Kurds will tell you that the Medes' priestly class were the 'Magi'. The Magi believed in a coming Saviour, born of a virgin, his conquest of Satan and his hosts, and the judgement of the world with fire. These were the same 'Magi' who were the first of all Gentiles to worship Christ.

Kurds – or Medes at any rate – were present at the Day of Pentecost and played a part in the early church. Many years later, they converted to Islam and the Magi class were extinguished.

Today, they number perhaps 25m people. Some are farmers or herders. Others work in cities across Europe. In the past two decades, Kurds have started to become Christians again, through a synergy of circumstances that has surprised observers – for example:

- They make up a disproportionate amount of the church in Turkey

- Some have responded to Christ in the 'Safe Haven' of northern Iraq as they have come into contact with Christian relief workers.[40]

The Persian world

NOWHERE QUITE LIKE IRAN

Iran is the last stop in our tour. And while culturally and historically there are many points of connection between Turkic Central Asia and Persian Central Asia, we have entered a different world. Here is some of the scenery:[41]

1 *Language:* People speaking the major languages of Iran, Afghanistan and Tajikistan (Farsi, Dari and Tajik) can understand each other. The Kurdish dialects and Pashto (also a language of Afghanistan) are close cousins. These languages are quite different from the Turkic family of languages – and incidentally, much closer to Indian and European languages.

2 *The Shi'a world:* Shi'ism is the smaller of the two portions into which Islam divided when there was a row over succession in its early days. Iran is the centre of Shi'ism. The Turkic world is mostly Sunni.

3 *The world of the Persian empires.* Persia has been a distinct empire for almost as long as the world has had empires. Wars between the Persians and the empires of the Mediterranean have been a feature of history for 2,500 years: Babylonians v Medo-Persians; Greeks v. Persians; Romans v. Parthians; Byzantines v. Sassanids; Ottomans v. Safavids. The Iraq/Iran war of the 1980s was a recent rumble on the same fault-line. The struggle between Saudi Arabia and Iran for leadership in the Muslim world is a further example.

4 *Sufism.* Sufism rejects the aloofness of God which is so central to Islam, and interprets the Qur'an mystically. Sufis consider their faith 'the religion of love' and 'the wine house' compared with the 'religion of law' you find in the mosque. Muslims ought to be grateful to Sufism for its inspiration in holding Islam together in the terrible days of the Mongol invasions, and for fuelling much Islamic missionary activity. Both Sunni and Shi'a Islam have produced forms of Sufism; but the great Sufi poets are Persian. Sufis typically have a high view of Jesus, his freedom, love, and union with God, regarding him as one of Sufism's 'perfect men'.

5 *One nation*. Iran, with a population of 68m, is a mosaic of ethnic groups. The Persians are the largest but other sizeable ones include the Azeris and the Kurds. However, Iran, throughout history has successfully welded its ethnic groups together into a united nation with a common language, a shared, old border, and an appetite for ethnic and religious tolerance.

Iranians, then, can be forgiven for thinking that they have deeper cultural roots, better poetry, a more elegant civilisation, a more settled national identity and a better spin on the Islamic traditions than any other part of the world. This same uniqueness has a flip side: a national sense of isolation and insecurity: Iran the good land, forever subverted by foreign intrigues. Various peoples over the years have received the blame for all Iran's troubles – among them Romans, Mongols, Turks, British, and Russians. The current incumbents are the Americans and Israelis.

As we might expect, Iran was also unique in the path it chose through the choppy waters of the 20th century. It tried the Turkish route from the 1920s but then in 1979 overthrew it with a radical Islamic revolution, one of the most dramatic changes of course for any country in the post-war period.

SHI'ISM

The Shi'a – Sunni split in Islam occurred after the assassination of the fourth Caliph, Ali, Muhammad's cousin and son-in-law. Shi'as (partisans) of Ali supported Ali's claim to the throne. Sunni's didn't.

Shi'a Islam has grown to differ from mainstream Sunni Islam. Within Shi'ism:

- Clerics have a more 'priestly' role.

- Law is different. For example Shi'ism includes the idea of temporary marriage contracts, by which a man may legally marry a woman for a fixed term, say a few months.

- Different anniversaries are celebrated. Central to Shi'a practice is the re-enactment of the martyrdom of Ali at the '10th of Muharram' every year.

This re-enactment can include wide-scale public weeping and breast-beating as a kind of annual catharsis of all one's personal griefs. Some strains of Shi'ite belief see Ali's martyrdom as almost a vicarious death for the sins of the world. The public displays of grief at the 10th of Muharram go a long way to explain the public scenes around the death, funeral and memorials of Ayatollah Khomeini, where people also take the opportunity to mourn and wail in the streets.

- Large Shi'ite groups also exist in South Asia and in the Lebanon. The Baha'i faith, which understands itself as a world faith and which is persecuted in Muslim lands as much as Christianity, is an offshoot of Shi'ism.

BIOGRAPHY OF A REVOLUTION

Iran's Islamic revolution brought militant Islam to the attention of the world's media in the 1980s and 1990s like nothing else. It was a story, above all, of accepted (Western) norms overthrown. Embassies were besieged. Child soldiers and women were recruited for the front lines in the Iraq/Iran war.[42] A novelist, Salman Rushdie, famously received death threats for poking a Qur'anic sore spot. International terror groups were sponsored. Probably nothing in recent years has given Islam such bad press as the Iranian Revolution.

Yet the Revolution had its roots in the unjust (but pro-Western) policies of the previous Shahs. These brought oil wealth and new freedoms to an elite, but also excluded many – too many:

- The religious leaders

- The *bazaaris* (members of the trade guilds who had been at the heart of Iranian commercial and political life for generations)

- The poor, who saw precious little oil wealth filter down to them through the canopy of corruption above.

Nor were the Shahs 'pro-Western' enough to embrace such ideas as democracy, freedom of speech, or the rights of minorities.

Into that context spoke Ayatollah Khomeini, then exiled in France,[43] using the subversive new technology of the cassette tape. He preached a return to the good old days of the Rightly Guided Caliphs (the Islamic leaders who presided over the original Muslim community in the few golden decades before it was rent by schism and corruption). He mixed that call with gestures to the far-left (throw off the foreign yoke, free the poor and the oppressed, let everyone enjoy the oil wealth).

Brought to power by street demonstrations, Khomeini then proceeded to eliminate his enemies and former allies one by one: first, the far left, then, his former comrades-in-arms the Mujahadeen. He surrounded the remaining apparatus of state with committees and guardians that delivered all ultimate power into his hands. By the time he was finished, Iran was a single-party police state, run by clerics with a worldview from the wrong millennium, with moral police enforcing clothing and courtship rules, and laws that took Iran's legal code back to mediaeval times.

Khomeini's death in 1989 removed the driver from the cab, and a revolutionary genius from the world, but the fearsome machine he built still rolls along.

EFFECTS OF A REVOLUTION

What is his legacy?

- *Worldwide fear:* What happened in Iran terrified governments around the world. The fear of an Islamic revolution lies at the back of political calculations made from Malaysia to India to Uzbekistan to Algeria – watch the way Islamists, usually by undemocratic means, are excluded from political power, suppressed, and sometimes jailed and killed.

In Iran itself the revolution cannot be called a success.

- *Power struggles:* Iran's politics at the moment is a story of the religious elite hanging on to power in the face of rejection and unpopularity from the masses. Real power still rests with unelected mullahs. Some Iranians see the elected president Khatami as a genuine reformer, others as the moderate face of an immoderate regime. All agree he has less power than his job title might suggest; he does not have hold of the steering wheel. Time will tell if Parliamentary elections in 2000 helped inch him towards real power.

- *Continuing bloodshed:* In 1998 the UN Commission on Human Rights condemned Iran's government for torturing and killing its citizens. In 1999, student demonstrators were shot. In the same year, a government official committed suicide after admitting his part in government-sponsored extra-judicial killings, including those of Christian leaders.

- *Grief:* The Iran-Iraq war, which was started by Saddam Hussain but exploited by the Iranian regime became for Iran like the First World War was for Europe. It filled the land with cemeteries, and decimated a generation, to little obvious point.

- *Emigration:* Iranians have been free to leave their country, and up to four million have chosen this path since the revolution – a huge migration.

- *Economic woes:* Many Iranians struggle to make ends meet. One sympathetic observer described Iranians thus: 'Life is unfair, nothing good can last, one's sole obligations are to self and family. To survive and prosper you need a combination of luck, connections, sharp wits and few principles.'[44]

- *Concealment.* Iranians have learnt to become skilful at being one thing when on public view in Iran, another when at home. Outwardly people conform. But, for example, in some parts of Tehran, when the working day is over, the Islamic dress is packed away; out of the cupboard come the illegal portable satellite dish or the video tapes.

- *Disillusionment:* Many Iranians today will tell you privately that the mullahs who are now in power have become as rich, corrupt and ruthless as the Shah whom they replaced. Many long for Iran to be friends with the world community again: Iranians are a tolerant, friendly lot and they do not see themselves as being the right sort of stuff for a pariah state. A number are disillusioned not just with the government but with Islam itself. One (obviously biased) Iranian Christian leader claimed that 'half of the population would desert Islam if they had the freedom to do so.'[45]

IRAN'S CHURCH

So much for the country. What of the church?

Start with the ancient traditional churches, those found among communities like the Armenians, Syrians and Assyrians within Iran. Like so many Christian communities in the Muslim world, these churches:

- Co-exist fairly peacefully with their Muslim neighbours, just as they have done for centuries.

- Could be said to be inward looking and culturally remote from the majority community.

- Sometimes suffer discrimination

- Are slowly drifting into oblivion, largely through emigration. Iran's traditional Christian population was 4% at the beginning of 20th century, 0.5% at the end. It may have been 25% when the Arab invaders first arrived near the end of the first millennium.

The toleration shown to the traditional Christian churches continued throughout the revolution. Christianity is one of Iran's four official faiths, and Christians can meet openly together to worship.

Christian groups also take part in national celebrations in Iran (which is more than can often be said about Muslim groups in, say, Britain). A Christian choir, for example, sang the old hymn 'Tell it to Jesus' to the assembled ranks of politicians and mullahs at the centenary of Khomeini's birth in 1999.

THE NEW CHURCHES

Iran had been relatively open to receiving missionaries for the best part of 200 years up until 1979, and it had received some illustrious ones. Henry Martyn, for example, translator of the Persian New Testament in 1811 was one of the great missionary linguists of all time.[46] In the Victorian era, Protestant missionaries started institutions and churches in Iran, though, as elsewhere, relatively few Muslims signed up to the Christian faith. Victorian mission work was characterised more by causing upheavals (for good or ill) in the traditional churches.

In the 20th century, pioneering figures like the American Dr William Miller had a huge influence; even though he saw relatively few people turn to Christ, he trained them well. Christian leaders discipled by Miller became a vital part of the infrastructure for what was to follow.

Still by 1979 there had been no decisive movement to Christ among the Muslim community. The revolution ended formal missionary work in Iran, though in the few years of anarchy that followed the Shah's overthrow there was freedom, for the brave, to sell Bibles and Christian writings. Many of these printed materials still circulate in Iran today.

REFUGEE CHURCHES

Out of the flood of refugees in the 1980s, many were welcomed and cared for by Christian humanitarian groups around the world. Thousands of these refugees have turned to Christ. Today you can find churches of Iranian former Muslims popping up in such unlikely places as Turkey, Pakistan, India as well as Western countries. Iranian Christians International (one of several groups that seek to network Iranian Christians together) counts 10–12,000 Iranian Christians from Muslim backgrounds among the former refugees.[47] (Other people, though, come up with significantly smaller numbers.)

Observers of the scene suggest a percentage of refugees fake a conversion experience, and exaggerate the religious persecution in Iran, the better to obtain asylum. That may be so. Many others have clearly found a genuine, living faith. All kinds of Iranians have become Christians: former Communists, former secularists, former zealous Muslims.

WITHIN IRAN

In the mid-1980s within Iran itself hundreds of people from Islamic backgrounds began turning to Christ. Even this small fracture in the Islamic community is something that had been seen rarely in all the years since the Arab conquests in the 8th century.

The reaction to this unprecedented leakage was brutal. In 1990, the Bible Society was closed down (always a bad sign since Bible societies are usually the most inoffensive of all Christian NGOs); church leaders were called in for questioning; restrictions were placed on church activities. The same year, shockingly, Hussain Soodmand, an Assemblies of God pastor who had led many Muslims to Christ, was executed.

Three years later another prominent leader, Mehdi Dibaj, after nine years in jail, was sentenced to death for 'apostasy' from Islam. His case was taken up and given worldwide publicity through the efforts of a colleague – the leader of the largest Protestant community in Iran – Haik Hovsepian-Mair. A Western media 'feeding frenzy' followed, leading to a dramatic week in 1994, in which Dibaj was suddenly freed from prison and Hovsepian-Mair was kidnapped, then murdered. A few months later Dibaj himself was killed. Shortly after Dibaj's death came the murder of Tateos Michaelian, a renowned scholar and translator, and a respected church leader.

It was a decapitation of the little Iranian Church, and it ended the few years in which Christians could openly help interested Muslims in Iran turn to Christ. At the same time, a number of the remaining Christian leaders realized it was time to leave their country. Since then, little, hard, publishable news has emerged from Iran. However:

- People who transmit radio programmes into Iran will tell you that thousands of people are listening to their broadcasts, and many of them show every sign of a deep, spiritual hunger – so much so that the radio broadcasters are now transmitting material suitable for building up 'radio churches' of people who have turned to Christ within Iran.

- Out of sight of the authorities, it may be that quiet Christian work is still going on, especially in smaller cells of people meeting in houses.[48]

- Iranians are still a tolerant people, and people who have turned to Christ and stayed out of the official gaze may find it quite possible to live quietly for Christ and meet with others who are doing the same thing. Some people brought to court accused of apostasy have been set free when they shared

---

SEEKER STORY

There was a man living in Tehran who had always wanted to find the truth. He never had any contact with committed Christians. He never heard the Gospel.

At death's door

Old age approached and he had a very serious stroke. He was rushed to hospital and was semi-conscious for three days. His family was by his bedside most of the time and his son was there day and night. The son longed for his father to say a few words.

The father never spoke, and after three days he died. From the human point of view he had known nothing about Christ. He was seemingly a 'lost' soul facing a Christless eternity.

The Jesus dream

A few days later the son had a vivid dream. His father came to him and spoke about those last days in the hospital. 'When I was in the hospital I saw Jesus. He told me He was the one I'd always been looking for. He told me He was the truth, and the only way to meet God was to believe in Him.'

So there, semi-conscious, this old man became a believer. Jesus didn't let him enter eternity alone.

The father went on in the dream to say sorry for not talking to the son – 'But for those three days, I was all the time with Jesus – that's why I couldn't talk to you.' The father's final words were – 'Go and tell the family about Jesus.'

The next morning the son was very excited but very nervous. What would the rest of the family say if he asked them to believe in Christ? With apprehension he sat down at the breakfast table. He noticed his younger sister wasn't there. When he asked where she was, they said she was upset.

So he went to get her. She was sitting on her bed, knees up, head down. As he knocked, she looked up, her eyes glistening with tears. He sat down and gently took her hand – 'What's the matter?'

'I've had a dream – but you'll be upset...' She looked at her brother, a little frightened...

'Don't worry – I won't get angry.' So she told him her story. They had both had the same dream!

All the members of this immediate family are now believers.[49]

testimony about how, for example, dreams or visions pointed them to Christ. At street level, in other words, persecution grinds to a halt in the face of the essential humanity of the Iranian people themselves.

The Iranian overseas groups are a fertile source of stories of what the gospel continues to do in Iran. Some of these groups have publicly claimed that there are as many new Christians within Iran as there are among Iranians overseas – in other words, thousands or even ten thousand or more. It's right to be very cautious about these estimates (the lack of hard facts encourages hype in some quarters, understatement in others).

But there's no smoke without fire: in a quarter-century of radical Islamic revolution the church among former Muslims has grown more than at any other quarter century in the past thousand years, a legacy that presumably Khomeini would not have wished for.

RESOURCES

BOOKS

Ron George
   1998 *The Spiritual Challenge of Modern Turkey* (UK: WIN International Associates).

Peter Hopkirk
   1980 *Foreign Devils on the Silk Road* (Oxford: OUP)

   1992 *The Great Game: The struggle for empire in Central Asia* (New York: Kodansha International)

Tim Kelsey
   1996 *Dervish: The Invention of Modern Turkey* (Harmondsworth, Middlesex, England: Hamish Hamilton)

David C Lewis
   2000 *After Atheism: Religion and Ethnicity in Russia and Central Asia.* (Surrey UK: Curzon Press).

Samuel H Moffett
   1998 *A History of Christianity in Asia: Beginnings to 1500* (US: Orbis Books).

GENERAL

www.brigada.org/today/articles/webmission.html is an excellent introduction to web-based missions resources. The best first stop I know for missions information. Regularly updated; more likely to be right than the rest of this resources page.

www.gmi.org is the home of overhead transparency maps, and the Electronic Operation World and much else.

www.global-prayer-digest.org is a daily prayer guide for the unreached, available via email or subscription.

www.calebproject.org Home to a movement in the US that seeks to mobilise students to serve among unreached peoples. Lots of helpful resources, particularly videos, booklets and prayer guides.

www.wec-int.org Home page for the mission agency WEC International with many useful links. Home also to the *Briefings* website.

www.answering-islam.org My favourite page for Muslim-Christian dialogue. Also includes a world of resources to explore, even much-needed religious humour pages. When it doesn't descend to ugliness, watching Muslims and Christians trying to convert each other is helpful for people of either faith or none.

PRAYER INFORMATION

Many of the individual partnerships are geared up to provide information for people wanting to invest some prayer into Central Asia. it. Much is semi-confidential, and not on the Web.

Some email addresses to start with, however are these:

Central Asia Partnership (AEMI) (This is the umbrella organization): ca@xc.org PO Box 210, West Drayton, Middlesex, UB7 8NN, UK

Tajik Partnership: 105645.3114@ compuserve.com

Tatar Partnership: TPNetwork@mail.com www.peopleteams.org/tatar

Also try: go@xc.org; 76145.1774@compuserve.com

Iranian partnerships

- Elam ministries helps network and train Iranian Christians, and communicate news of the work of God among Iranians to other Christians. 'Grenville', Grenville Rd, Shackleford, Godalming, Surrey GU8 6AX, England.

- www.Farsinet.com is the home page for all things Persian and Farsi. Iranian Christians International (ICIinc@compuserve.com) and Persian World Outreach (Persianwo@csi.com) can be found from this page.

Business ventures

The Business Professional Network can link groups of business people with entrepreneurs in Central Asia. It has a track record in facilitating the creation of small and medium-sized businesses in the former Communist world (news@bpn.org).

BOOKLETS, ETC

I know of two booklets in the popular 30-day prayer guide format:

Praying along the Silk Road
A short guide to all the countries mentioned in this book, available from this address: cafmc@holmsted.org.uk

30 Days of prayer for the Uyghurs
Excellent guide focussing on the Uyghurs of Western China and Kazakhstan available from RUN Ministries (102047.2422@compuserve.com).

The AD2000 and Beyond networking movement has produced a glossy guide to the Turkic peoples called *The 35/45 Turkic Window* (info@ad2000.org; www.ad2000.org).

Elam Review is an occasional magazine on things Persian, available from Elam ministries.

NOTES

1 See Peter Hopkirk, *Foreign Devils on the Silk Road* (Oxford: OUP 1980) p 14–16.

2 Stephen Neill, *A History of Christian Missions* (Harmondsworth, Middlesex: Penguin Books 1964) , p 95.

3 Rabban Sauma, quoted by Stephen Neill *op. cit.*, p 125.

4 Central Asia's Christians were Assyrians, part of the Assyrian Church of the East (also known, though ACE Christians do not like the term today, as 'Nestorians'). They were counted heretical by most of the rest of Christendom because of disagreements over the nature, or natures, of Christ, dating back to the Church Councils of Ephesus (431) and Chalcedon (451).

5 Neill, *op. cit*, p 133.

6 Peter Hopkirk *The Great Game: The Struggle for Empire in Central Asia* (New York: Kodansha International 1992), p 5.

7 By globalisation we mean, crudely, the way that technology and economics are changing the world's cultures and causing them to impinge on each other to an ever-greater degree. It is a process that his been going on since at least the Industrial Revolution. While globalisation has great potential for both good and harm, it is always destructive of old ways and thus perceived as a threat in many cultures.

8 *Time* magazine 7/6/96 talked of 'children with no eyes, grossly oversize heads, a rate of deformed babies 3 or 4 times the norm.'

9 See for example 'Poisoned Island' in *The Economist*, 10th July 1999.

10 An alternative explanation is that after the first generation of Communist radicals passed from the scene, the traditional conservatism of the Central Asian peoples re-asserted itself.

11 Most of this data was extracted, with some changes, from a privately published information leaflet. The population numbers are taken from the 13th edition of the *Ethnologue* (1999: see www.sil.org), and are the numbers of people who speak the mother tongue(s) associated with that ethnic group.

12 Communities of Tatars are also found in Bulgaria, China, Kazakhstan, Romania, Turkey, and Uzbekistan.

13 According to Luis Bush, *The 35/45 Turkic Window* (brochure published in 1999 by the AD2000 and Beyond Movement, www.ad2000.org).

14 Glenn Myers *The World Christian Starter Kit* (3rd Edition 1993. UK: WEC Publications and US: Operation Mobilization Literature Ministry)

15 Luis Bush counted 1600 Turkic believers at the beginning of the 1990s. Fifteen hundred of these came from the three Turkic peoples who started to respond to Christ rather sooner than the rest: the Gaugaz

(who were already nominally Christian) the Millet of Bulgaria, and the Turks of Turkey.

16 See Peter Hopkirk, *Foreign Devils on the Silk Road*, p 214.

17 Mildred Cable and Francesca French's books can often be hunted down in second-hand bookshops or the attics of elderly relatives (at least in the UK).

18 Though being narrowed by Communist progress in education and assimilation.

19 Quoted in *Kazakhs Search For Identity* published by the Caleb project, August 1992. (For more details on the Caleb project, see www.calebproject.org.)

20 Quoted from an Open Doors guide, *20 Key Points to Pray for Uzbekistan*, November 1993

21 When I asked my source to check out the story I told here, he wrote the following: 'It was told me by a Pentecostal church leader from the town where this Imam was said to be converted. I checked with another underground church leader who works predominantly in the same region and he had not heard of the story. This isn't surprising as Pentecostals (AoG), Baptists, Korean Presbyterian and "Independents" are not unified and don't usually share information.'

22 Correspondence with the author, May 2000.

23 These are by no means the only challenges, of course. The great challenge, as everywhere in the world, is to produce healthy, well-taught, growing churches full of Christ-like individuals, who then change the world. This could be broken down into many individual needs: prayer, holiness, revival; leadership training, media, arts and literature work; and so on. In this chapter we are just highlighting some current issues that are special to the Central Asian scene.

24 Mehrdad Haghayeghi: 'Islamic Revival in the Central Asian Republics', *Central Asian Survey* (1994) 13 (2) pp, 249–266.

25 In 1995, for example, the Uzbek government closed down the Andizhan mosque in eastern Uzbekistan. Its local imam disappeared shortly afterwards (*Economist*, February 21st 1998, p 78).

26 Jurg Opprecht of the Business Professional Network (email: info@bpn.org).

27 Galatians, Ephesians, Colossians, 1 and 2 Timothy, Philemon, 1 and 2 Peter and Revelation were all explicitly addressed to believers in what is now Turkey.

28 See F F Bruce *The Spreading Flame* (The Paternoster Church History Volume I) (Paternoster, Exeter, UK: 1958), pp 169–171. The classical reference is *Epistles of Pliny*, X, 96 and 97.

29 I found this quote from '*The Challenge of Turkey Today*' a brochure published by mission agency Operation Mobilisation. I'm grateful to that brochure both for this quote and for its excellent overview of Turkish Christian history.

30 F F Bruce *op. cit.*, p 174.

31 Bernard Lewis *The Middle East* (London, Weidenfeld & Nicholson 1995), p 115.

32 OM's leaflet *The Challenge of Turkey Today*.

33 Interestingly, some Armenians in Turkey experienced a Pentecostal awakening some years before the genocide. They were prophetically warned to leave Turkey. Some did, and found their way to Los Angeles. Already familiar with such spiritual manifestations as prophecy, tongues, and healing, they helped strengthen the Azusa Street revival, from which the world-wide Pentecostal/Charismatic awakening sprang.

34 Quoted in Tim Kelsey *Dervish: The Invention of Modern Turkey*, London: Hamish Hamilton 1996, p 30.

35 See David Zeidan's article 'The Alevi of Anatolia' in *Middle East Review of International Affairs*, Vol 3, No 1, December 1999. (www.biu.ac.il/SOC/besa/meria/journal/1999/issue4/jv3n4a5.html)

36 Ron George claims: 'Turkey denies that the Armenian genocides ever happened and until this truth is faced and confessed a great weight of guilt and denial hangs round the nation causing much darkness.' (*The Spiritual Challenge of Modern Turkey: WIN International Associates*, UK p 40).

37 See, for example, Romans 1:14.

38 *The Challenge of Turkey Today*, leaflet from Operation Mobilisation

39 See 2 Kings 17:6.

40 For more on the Kurds see two articles by Matthew Hand: 'The Modern Descendants of the Magi Seek the Saviour: The Kurds' *World Christian* (no date given in my source but likely to be 1992–1994) and 'The Kurds, a prophetic people' in the UK-based magazine *Prophecy Today* Vol 12, No. 6, Nov/Dec 1996.

41 I'm grateful to an unpublished report by David Zeidan for much of this information.

42 1 million people died in the Iraq/Iran war, of whom 90,000 were soldiers under the age of 15.

43 After many years' exile in Iraq.

44 David Zeidan.

45 Abe Ghaffari of the agency Iranian Christians International agency, quoted in the email newsletter *FRIDAYFax* Vol 99, No. 43, October 29th, 1999.

46 In his short career, Martyn, a prize-winning mathematician, had already translated the New Testament into Urdu and would go on to revise the Arabic New Testament.

47 See their website www.Farsinet.com/ici

48 Though there are Farsi-speaking churches meeting openly in Tehran, the government does not allow inquirers from a Muslim background to attend these services.

49 The source for this story requested anonymity, but is reliable.

FOR PRAYER

The last decade or two has seen an unprecedented number of Central Asian people turn to Christ from an Islamic background. This has happened right across the Turkic and Persian worlds, from Bulgaria to Xinjiang, from Iran to Tajikistan. The detail of the story has been different in every place, but the outcome has always been the same. This movement has only involved a tiny percentage of the population. But – in its extent, and in the way movements to Christ have happened across the region from a previously unyielding background – it is unique.

Not all the good beginnings of Church history lead anywhere. The events of the 1980s and 1990s across Central Asia may prove to be just a blip – an obscure consequence, perhaps, of the end of the Cold War. Or, they may prove to be the start of a long trend which sees the Christian Church eventually move from the margins to being the heart of these countries, much as the Early Church eventually did.

For the leaders of these countries, as religious freedoms become challenged again.

✧ ✧ ✧

For the young churches within these cultures that they will grow like Jesus did – in stature, in wisdom, in favour with God and people.

✧ ✧ ✧

For the church leaders, some of whom are local people, others who are expatriate Christians, that they will become excellent shepherds of their 'flocks'.

✧ ✧ ✧

For the outside Christian agencies, for their continued fruitful cooperation.

✧ ✧ ✧

For the many people, especially outside the larger cities, who have no churches anywhere near them.